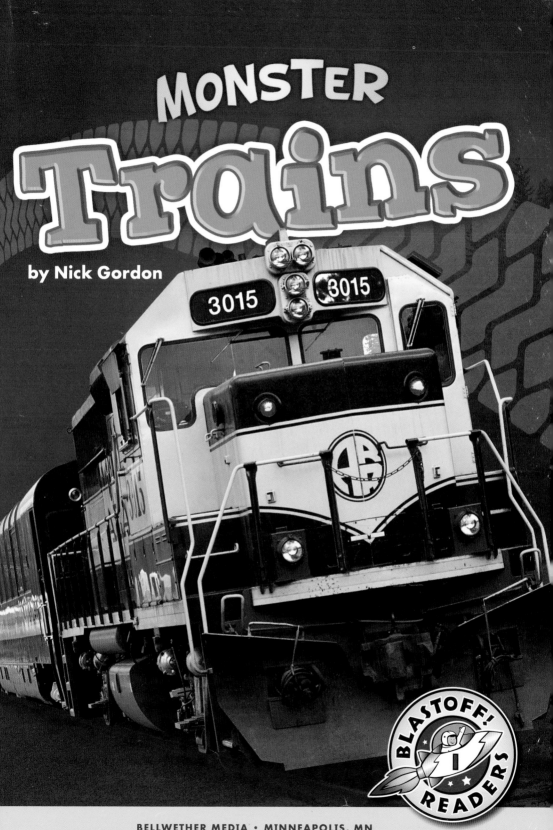

MONSTER
Trains

by Nick Gordon

3015 3015

BELLWETHER MEDIA · MINNEAPOLIS, MN

Note to Librarians, Teachers, and Parents:

Blastoff! Readers are carefully developed by literacy experts and combine standards-based content with developmentally appropriate text.

Level 1 provides the most support through repetition of high-frequency words, light text, predictable sentence patterns, and strong visual support.

Level 2 offers early readers a bit more challenge through varied simple sentences, increased text load, and less repetition of high-frequency words.

Level 3 advances early-fluent readers toward fluency through increased text and concept load, less reliance on visuals, longer sentences, and more literary language.

Level 4 builds reading stamina by providing more text per page, increased use of punctuation, greater variation in sentence patterns, and increasingly challenging vocabulary.

Level 5 encourages children to move from "learning to read" to "reading to learn" by providing even more text, varied writing styles, and less familiar topics.

Whichever book is right for your reader, Blastoff! Readers are the perfect books to build confidence and encourage a love of reading that will last a lifetime!

This edition first published in 2014 by Bellwether Media, Inc.

No part of this publication may be reproduced in whole or in part without written permission of the publisher. For information regarding permission, write to Bellwether Media, Inc., Attention: Permissions Department, 5357 Penn Avenue South, Minneapolis, MN 55419.

Library of Congress Cataloging-in-Publication Data

Gordon, Nick.
  Monster trains / by Nick Gordon.
    pages cm. – (Blastoff! readers: Monster machines)
  Summary: "Developed by literacy experts for students in kindergarten through grade three, this book introduces extreme trains to young readers through leveled text and related photos"–Provided by publisher.
  Audience: K-3.
  Includes bibliographical references and index.
  ISBN 978-1-60014-939-9 (hardcover : alk. paper)
  1. Railroad trains–Juvenile literature. 2. Railroads–Juvenile literature. I. Title.
  TF148.G67 2014
  385–dc23
                                                                    2013002286

Printed in the United States of America, North Mankato, MN.

Table of Contents

Monster Trains!

Trains can have hundreds of **cars**. Some trains are a **mile** long.

Their powerful **locomotives** pull heavy loads.

Trains zip along **tracks** at fast speeds.

tracks

Heavy Loads

Freight trains carry the heaviest loads.

These trains
often move coal
or **iron ore**.

coal

Long Railways

Passenger trains move on long **railways**. Some travel thousands of miles.

The Trans-Siberian Railway is the longest in the world.

Trans-Siberian Railway

High Speeds

Some trains race at high speeds. They are called bullet trains.

The ICE 3 is a bullet train. It travels over 185 miles (300 kilometers) per hour!

ICE 3

Glossary

cars—vehicles pulled by a train; cars carry people, animals, or goods.

freight trains—trains that carry goods

iron ore—rock made up of a metal called iron

locomotives—parts of trains that provide power to pull the cars

mile—a distance equal to four times around a football field

passenger trains—trains that take people from place to place

railways—sets of tracks that are connected over long distances

tracks—the paths on which trains run

To Learn More

AT THE LIBRARY

Bergin, Mark. *Trains*. New York, N.Y.: Gareth Stevens Publishing, 2013.

Doeden, Matt. *Trains*. Mankato, Minn.: Capstone Press, 2007.

Shields, Amy. *Trains*. Washington, D.C.: National Geographic, 2011.

ON THE WEB
Learning more about trains is as easy as 1, 2, 3.

1. Go to www.factsurfer.com.

2. Enter "trains" into the search box.

3. Click the "Surf" button and you will see a list of related Web sites.

With factsurfer.com, finding more information is just a click away.

Index

The images in this book are reproduced through the courtesy of: Ruth Peterkin, front cover; Mayskyphoto, pp. 4-5; Albert Pego, pp. 6-7; Tomas Anderson/ Glow Images, pp. 8-9; Peter Gudella, p. 9 (small); Dave Reede/ Getty Images, pp. 10-11; Robert McGuoey/ Glow Images, pp. 12-13; Leonid Andronov, pp. 14-15; Bigmax, pp. 16-17; JTB Photo Communications, Inc./ Age Fotostock, pp. 18-19; Warter/ Associated Press, pp. 20-21.